SECOND NATURE
CHANGES & CHALLENGES IN THE NEW ENVIRONMENT

Extreme Environments
LIVING ON THE EDGE

By Amy Tilmont and Jeff Garside
with Mark Stewart

NORWOOD HOUSE PRESS

All photos are courtesy of Getty Images, except for the following:
Photo credits: Deposit Photos (7, 9, 14, 16, 21, 26); Patrick Blanc (32); Kip Evans (35);
James Burling Chase (43); National Aeronautics and Space Administration (41).
Cover Photo: Marco Tortonese

Special thanks to Content Consultant Ashley McDowell.

Library of Congress Cataloging-in-Publication Data

Tilmont, Amy.
  Extreme environments : living on the edge / by Amy Tilmont, Jeff Garside,
Mark Stewart.
    p. cm. -- (Second nature)
  Includes bibliographical references and index.
  Summary: "From desert villagers to tube worms clustered around ocean
vents, life has a remarkable way of surviving and thriving in the most
challenging of places. This book looks at how humans and animals have
evolved to flourish in the unlikeliest locations...and at just how fragile
these fringe ecosystems can be"--Provided by publisher.
  ISBN-13: 978-1-59953-458-9 (library edition : alk. paper)
  ISBN-10: 1-59953-458-4 (library edition : alk. paper)
1. Biotic communities--Juvenile literature. 2. Adaptation
(Biology)--Juvenile literature. 3. Evolution (Biology)--Juvenile
literature. I. Garside, Jeff. II. Stewart, Mark, 1960- III. Title.
  QH541.14.T55 2011
  577.5'8--dc23

                                        2011017629

Manufactured in the United States of America in North Mankato, Minnesota.
176N—072011

COVER: Few environments are as extreme as the South Pole.
This photo was taken at the McMurdo station in Antarctica.

Contents

1 What's the Problem? 4

2 How We Got Here 14

3 If We Do Nothing 22

4 Bright Ideas 28

5 Trailblazers 34

6 Field Tested 36

7 Career Opportunities 38

8 Expert Opinions 42

9 What Can I Do? 44

Glossary 46

Sources & Resources 47

Index & Authors 48

Words in **bold type** are defined on page 46.

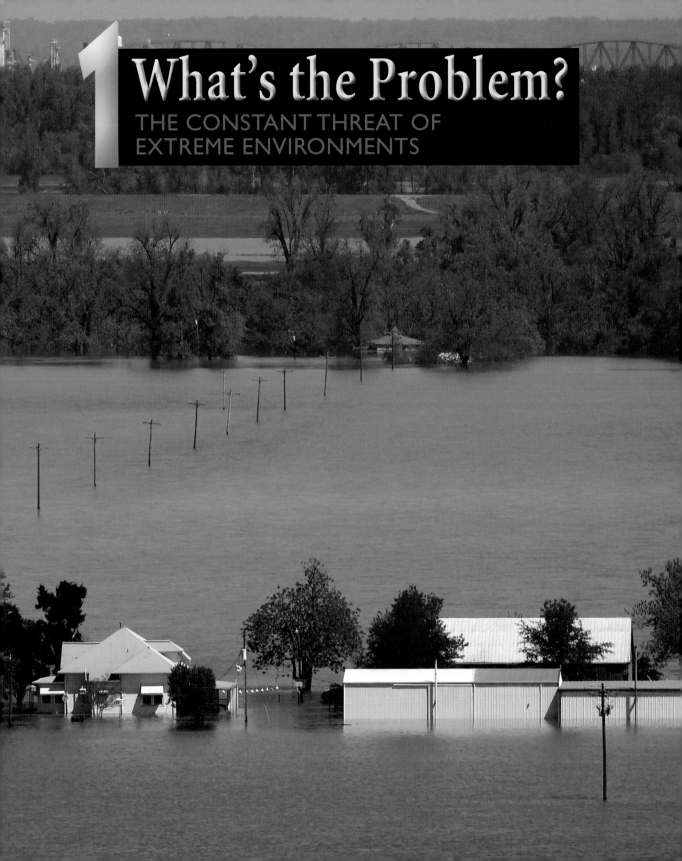

1 What's the Problem?
THE CONSTANT THREAT OF EXTREME ENVIRONMENTS

When you think of a small town in the United States, do you think of an extreme environment? Probably not. But nature is unpredictable. There is always the chance that a friendly environment can turn unfriendly in a hurry.

In the spring of 2011, people living along the Mississippi River watched in disbelief as the Army Corps of Engineers blew up the Birds Point levee in southern Illinois. A levee is an earthen mound that keeps a river from overflowing its banks. When the Birds Point levee was destroyed, millions of gallons of water gushed into the surrounding farmland. More than 100,000 acres were affected. The people living on these farms had time to get away. But any creature that could not run, crawl, slither, or fly away fast enough drowned.

Why did the government have to make this heartbreaking decision? Weeks of rain had caused the Mississippi River to rise to dangerous levels. Downstream from Birds Point, the city of Cairo would have been overwhelmed if the rising waters had no place to go. Many other towns would have faced the same fate. The choice

Weather can change instantly and turn any town into an extreme environment. That's what happened to some people in Illinois in 2011.

was made to sacrifice a few farms and wildlife to save more people and property further downstream.

Compared to the people of Pakistan, neighbors of the Mississippi were lucky. In the summer of 2010, **monsoon** rains were much heavier than usual in the region. The Indus River overflowed its banks. About one-fifth of the country was under water. The government did not move quickly enough to warn everyone. More than 2,000 people were swept away.

Extreme environments are places where conditions would kill almost every life form. They exist all over the world. In some of these places, living things—including humans—have adapted and learned to thrive. In others, the habitat is so harsh that only very specialized life forms can survive. None of this surprises scientists. But they are worried that extreme environments may be growing in size and becoming more destructive. That has led them to ask: Is human activity making the world a more dangerous place?

TOO EXTREME FOR PEOPLE

Humans like to believe they can control their environment, no matter how extreme. Often just the opposite is true. One look at the world's harshest **ecosystems** shows why. The two most common factors that make environments extreme are climate and elevation. Places that are very hot or very cold demand

The Atacama Desert is one of the most unforgiving climates in the world.

that people and animals adapt in order to survive. In northern Ethiopia, the average high temperature is 106° F (41° C). At that temperature, it is almost impossible for humans to survive. There are many abandoned towns in this region, including Dallol, which has been called the hottest place on earth.

Why would people have ever lived in Dallol? Under the ground, there were valuable deposits of salt. Mining this resource was good business. But as technology improved elsewhere in the world, the mines of Dallol closed. There were a lot more places to mine salt that were much more conducive to human life.

In Chile, the Atacama Desert is the driest place on earth. It receives less than a tenth of an inch of rain every year. Parts of the desert look like the surface of Mars. Yet people have been trying to live in the Atacama for centuries. They get their water from tiny oases. It limits the population to just a few hundred people in some places. Why don't they move? The simple answer is some people find that this climate suits their lifestyles. For them, the Atacama Desert is home.

Atacama is not very friendly to animals, either. Over time, some animals have evolved to live on almost no water at all. For example, Atacama's largest **arthropod** is the scorpion. Desert lizards and a bird called a passerine also survive in Atacama because they hunt scorpions. A few mammals live there also. Species of mouse and fox are sometimes seen. All of these creatures survive on the tiny amount of moisture available.

Life in polar regions—areas of extreme cold—can be even more dangerous to humans. Water is not an issue there. The land is covered with ice and snow. The problem is that, in almost every way, people are tropical animals. Our bodies are not built for dealing with extreme cold temperatures. Early humans learned to survive far from the equator only after they began making warm clothing, building shelters, and controlling fire.

Why did early humans move into cold-weather climates? Because their food supply was there. They hunted mammoths and other beasts through the ice and snow in order to eat. People learned to survive by respecting the dangers of the environment and also by learning from the animals that lived there. Today, humans live in extreme cold mainly for economic reasons, such as the opportunity to get a high-paying job or buy an inexpensive home. In addition, some people go to these areas to study them.

Chernobyl

What is the effect on wildlife from nuclear accidents? In 1986, a plant in Chernobyl, Ukraine, exploded. So much radiation leaked out that more than 350,000 people had to move away. In the years following the accident, some environmental scientists began studying the region around Chernobyl. They found that many animals died or failed to reproduce. Others gave birth to babies with deformities due to the radiation. They discovered high levels of radiation in fish living in nearby rivers, too.

Twenty-five years later, the scientists found something else. The Chernobyl nuclear plant is still smoldering. Radiation levels are still high in many of the animals living nearby. Yet the local wildlife has bounced back. Wild boars have moved into abandoned homes. Rare species of wild horses and lynx are plentiful. Birds and bats have turned old buildings into mass roosting areas. Despite the radiation, animals are clearly doing better since people have moved away.

Trees in the area have not done as well. Many have bizarre, twisted shapes. This is one of the effects of radiation. It has confused the chemical signals that tell trees which direction to grow.

As this abandoned building shows, Chernobyl has become a ghost town. Buildings in the surrounding area look much the same inside.

MAN-MADE EXTREMES

Sometimes when humans try to control their environment, it becomes "extreme" overnight. For example, the city of New Orleans, Louisiana, was founded in the 1700s on hills overlooking the Mississippi River. As the city expanded, people needed safe places to live. The surrounding swamps were drained, and houses were built on the dry land. In order to protect the growing city, a system of levees was built to keep the Mississippi from overflowing into these neighborhoods—many of which were below the level of the river.

No one thought of New Orleans as an extreme environment until 2005. That summer, Hurricane Katrina slammed into the Louisiana coast. The powerful storm pushed water up the Mississippi, where it met the water flowing down from the north. The pressure burst the levees, and the low-lying areas of New Orleans flooded. More than 1,500 people drowned—some in their attics, trying to escape the rising water.

People living on the northeast coast of Japan did not think they lived in an extreme environment, either. In fact, many Japanese took their vacations in this beautiful part of the country. They did not worry that Japan sits atop the "Ring of Fire"—a horseshoe-shaped area where earthquakes are common. In early March 2011, a powerful quake shook this part of Japan. It was followed by a tsunami that killed more than 20,000 people along the Japanese coastline.

The destruction after the earthquake and tsunami in Japan left thousands of people homeless.

Though the buildings in Japan were built to withstand natural disasters, many collapsed because the earthquake was so powerful. Towns along the coast had constructed large seawalls to protect them from tsunamis. These structures barely slowed the giant waves.

Japan's natural disaster alarmed people for another reason. A nuclear power plant in Fukushima was damaged during the earthquake. The tsunami prevented crucial safety systems from working correctly. Fires and explosions followed, and large amounts of radiation were released into the environment. The government ordered citizens living within 12 miles (19.3 kilometers) of the power plant to move away. Tests on food and water as far as 30 miles (48.3 kilometers) away showed signs of contamination. Months after the accident, radiation was still entering the air, land, and water. Sadly, this environment now may be "extreme" for generations.

WORLD VIEW

One way to measure extreme environmental conditions is to track high and low temperatures. If a certain area shows a pattern of unusual heat or cold, scientists may be able to predict a change in weather. From there, they can work to find out what may be causing that change. This information can also help people, animals, and plants adapt to their surroundings.

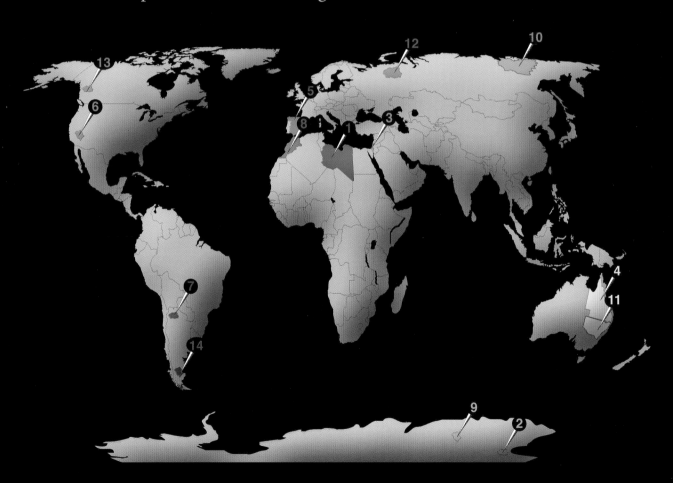

Temperature Extremes

	CONTINENT	RECORD HIGHEST	LOCATION
1	Africa	136° F / 58°C	El Azizia, Libya
2	Antarctica	59°F / 15°C	Vanda Station
3	Asia	129°F / 54°C	Tirat Tsvi, Israel
4	Australia	128°F / 53°C	Cloncurry, Queensland
5	Europe	122°F / 50°C	Seville, Spain
6	North America	134°F / 57°C	Death Valley, CA
7	South America	120°F / 49°C	Rivadavia, Argentina

	CONTINENT	RECORD LOWEST	LOCATION
8	Africa	-11°F / -24°C	Ifrane, Morocco
9	Antarctica	-129°F / -89°C	Vostok Station
10	Asia	-90°F / -68°C	Oymyakon, Russia
11	Australia	-9°F / -23°C	Charlotte Pass, NSW
12	Europe	-67°F / -55°C	Ust-Shchuger, Russia
13	North America	-81°F / -63°C	Snag, Yukon, Canada
14	South America	-27°F / -33°C	Sarmiento, Argentina

These temperatures were recorded between 1881 and 2008.

Source of data is National Climatic Data Center (NCDC)
and National Oceanic and Atmospheric Administration (NOAA).

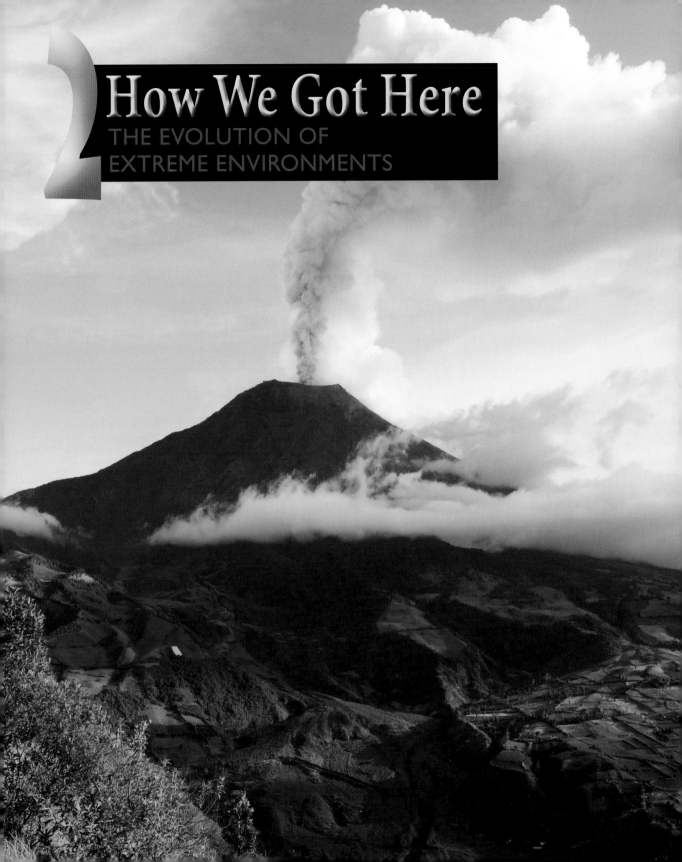

2 How We Got Here
THE EVOLUTION OF EXTREME ENVIRONMENTS

Since the beginning of life on earth, every type of organism has had to develop in response to its environment. If it doesn't, it will perish. The more extreme the environment, the more extreme the response. The result of this process is greater **biodiversity**. In fact, geologists and biologists believe that life began in an environment so extreme that it is difficult for us to imagine that anything could survive.

Between 3.5 and 4 billion years ago, the earth had cooled enough to form a rocky crust. Volcanic eruptions blasted water vapor, carbon, hydrogen, oxygen, nitrogen, and other gases into the atmosphere. These gases combined to make simple **organic** compounds. Over tens of millions of years, the water vapor and organic compounds condensed and formed ancient oceans. In this soupy mix were the building blocks of life.

The Tungurahua volcano in Ecuador is still active. Volcanic eruptions billions of years ago created conditions suitable for living things.

Dinosaurs that looked like this replica once ruled the earth.

How the first single-cell organism sprang to life is unclear. Did it happen in an undersea vent? Did life begin in a shallow pond under layers of clay? Did some event we do not fully understand "ignite" life somewhere? Scientists have been trying to test a number of theories. So far they have been unable to answer this question.

RISE OF MAMMALS

How humans evolved dates back to the extreme environment created by an asteroid impact 65 million years ago. At that time, dinosaurs were the dominant species on earth. When the asteroid struck, it unleashed huge amounts of energy. The environment turned deadly for dinosaurs. Those that were too large to take shelter were burned by firestorms. The material created by the asteroid's impact blew high into the sky and blotted out the sun, killing surface plants. Dinosaurs that fed on plants had little to eat and died out. The meat-eating dinosaurs soon had no plant eaters to feed on, and they died out, too.

When dinosaurs became extinct, mammals had the opportunity they needed. Small, furry creatures had existed during the reign of the dinosaurs. They spent most of their time hiding underground, trying not to get eaten. Fortunately, underground was just the place to be after the asteroid struck!

It took another 10 million years for mammals to truly take over. Because mammals used up more oxygen than the dinosaurs did, they needed an oxygen-rich atmosphere to grow large. Fossil evidence shows that these conditions were present 55 million years ago, during the Eocene epoch. The earth's oceans—particularly the Atlantic (which was getting wider during the Eocene epoch)—may have doubled the amount of oxygen in the air.

THE BOTTLENECK

Fast-forward to 70,000 years ago. Among the mammals roaming the planet was a population of early humans in Africa. They numbered in the hundreds of thousands—possibly more. Scientists believe that a volcanic eruption in Indonesia led to **climate change**. This devastated the plant and animal species that humans relied upon for food. Some evidence suggests that this condition may have lasted for a century or more.

Most human ancestors could not adapt to the extreme challenges they faced and were wiped off the face of the earth. Those that survived competed for limited resources, which created a situation that **anthropologists** call a "bottleneck." Early humans were forced to invent new

A museum exhibit shows how Neanderthals lived thousands of years ago.

technologies and **rituals** that kept them one step ahead of nature. Of course, it is impossible to say exactly what happened or when it happened. However, we do know that everyone on earth is related to this small group of survivors. The population of humans recovered quickly after the climate returned to normal. Soon, modern humans were moving with great speed and confidence all over the globe.

In many of the places they explored, these migrating people encountered a species closely related to humans, the Neanderthal. Neanderthals and modern humans lived side by side for thousands of years. They competed for resources and may have fought each other. That changed with the dawn of the Ice Age about 40,000 years ago. Ice and snow covered large parts of the earth. Humans and

Neanderthals survived this extreme environment using different skills and technologies.

Neanderthals hunted in large hunting parties, often trapping creatures in the thick forests and stabbing them at close range. Humans developed weapons such as throwing spears and arrows. This enabled them to hunt in smaller groups and at a safer distance in open spaces. When the glaciers receded, there were more open spaces and fewer dense forests. Humans thrived, while Neanderthals struggled and eventually died out. Once again, the environment worked in our favor.

HUMANS AT THEIR WORST

Thousands of years later, we saw how environments are put at risk when humans make extremely bad decisions. The Fertile Crescent in the Middle East is one of the first places people began living in large cities. Three mighty rivers—The Tigris, the Euphrates, and the Jordan—flow through this region. People had enough water to drink and grow food because they managed the rivers well. They built levees to prevent flooding and **irrigation** canals to bring water to their fields during droughts.

This arrangement worked well for more than 2,500 years. Civilizations came and went—the Sumerians, the Babylonians, and the Parthians lived well in the Fertile Crescent. All understood the importance of repairing and maintaining the water systems. But in the 1200s, the rulers

PIG STORY

The first explorers were amazed at the large settlements Native Americans had built in North and South America. During the 1500s, Spanish explorers had the habit of releasing pigs into an ecosystem before they moved on. Because pigs breed quickly, they knew that there would be plenty of meat for the colonists that followed. But those colonists often found empty towns and villages.

Without realizing it, the Spaniards had turned a delicately balanced environment into an extreme one for the people who lived there. A group of wild pigs could destroy a village's crops in a matter of hours. The native people did not know how to stop them. Pigs also share some diseases with humans. They may have passed illnesses from the Spaniards to the Native Americans.

of the lands between the Tigris and Euphrates rivers failed to maintain them. The irrigation system slowly collapsed, and the cities disappeared. Since the 1400s, a large part of this region has been a desert.

Modern farming and **water management** technology is now available to correct the mistakes of the past. However, instead of getting better, the problem in the Fertile Crescent has worsened. Satellite images taken in 2001 of Iraq and Iran showed that only around 10 percent of the original ecosystem remains. Dams and drainage projects have turned the marshes near the Tigris and Euphrates rivers into salt-encrusted desert. The birds, plants, animals, and people that once enjoyed life there are almost all gone now. In this case, human activity turned thriving ecosystems into an extreme environment.

The Mayans

Throughout history, humans have found different ways to alter their environment. Often it has been for the better. Sometimes it has been for the worse. In one case, the result was so extreme that people had no choice but to simply walk away. This is what archaeologists believe happened to the Mayans, who built a great civilization in the jungles of present-day Mexico, Guatemala, Honduras, Belize, and El Salvador. They created large cities and had their own written language. Their civilization thrived for more than 1,000 years.

The Mayans constructed their cities around huge, stepped pyramids. They coated many of their buildings with **limestone**, which they painted with colorful symbols and designs. When new rulers took over, they often ordered structures to be rebuilt in their honor. Making that much limestone requires a tremendous amount of heat. The Mayans cut down a huge number of trees to build the fires they needed. Over the centuries, this may have triggered an ecological disaster. At some point, the environment could not support the cities. The Mayan civilization collapsed, and the people created their own small villages instead.

Many Mayan pyramids such as this one are still standing. Ironically, they may have played a part in the culture's downfall.

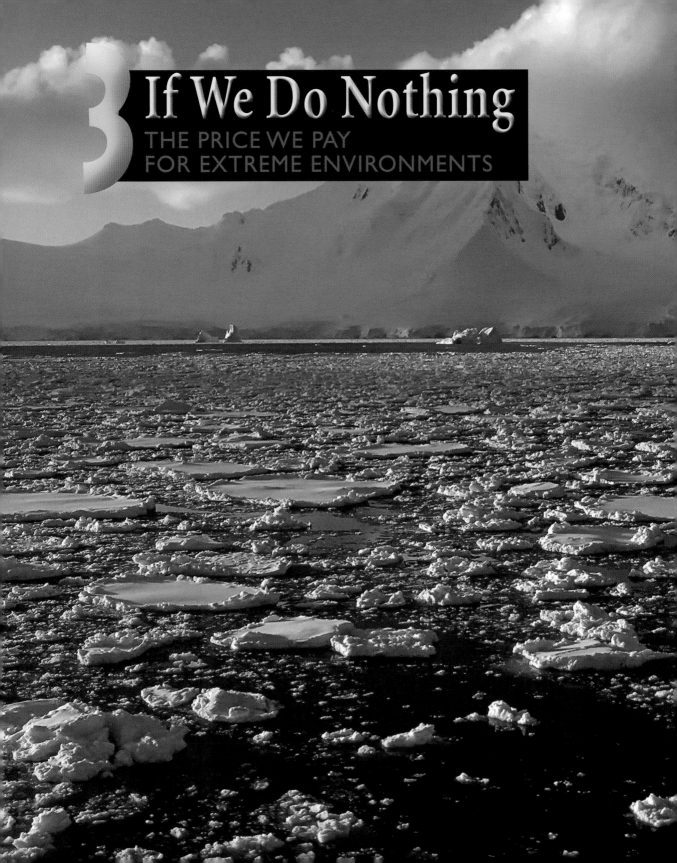

3 If We Do Nothing
THE PRICE WE PAY
FOR EXTREME ENVIRONMENTS

There is an old saying that knowledge is power. In the case of extreme environments, the more we understand about them, the better off we are. For example, enormous changes are happening to earth's most extreme environment, Antarctica, which is a desert environment in the coldest of temperatures. (Deserts exist in frigid climates, too.) Every year, more than 20 cubic miles (83.4 cubic kilometers) of ice disappears. Most scientists believe the cause is global warming. What they cannot explain is why the ice is disappearing from the eastern edge of Antarctica but not the western edge. Temperatures at the eastern edge of the continent are actually cooler than they are in the west.

What really has scientists scratching their heads is why a piece of ice the size of a small country broke off and floated away from Antarctica in 2010. Now they wonder how it will affect weather systems and ocean patterns. Scientists will also be watching a colony of Empire penguins, which may have to travel much farther to find food.

THE CONVEYOR BELT

If the dramatic changes in Antarctica are a result of human activity, doing nothing could be catastrophic.

From 2000 to 2010, the ice cap at the Arctic shrank by nearly 30 percent. A smaller ice cap reflects less sunlight, which could contribute to global warming.

Rising temperatures in the Arctic may pose another problem. A huge amount of carbon dioxide (CO_2) is locked in the region's permafrost, soil that remains frozen all year. When permafrost thaws, it releases CO_2 into the atmosphere. CO_2 is a greenhouse gas that contributes to global warming. In 2009, scientists studying permafrost reported that it contained three times the amount of CO_2 than had been previously estimated. If the permafrost melts, it will release more than a billion tons of CO_2 into the atmosphere each year—about four times more than all of the automobiles in the United States!

Scientists worry that adding too much cold, fresh water to ocean currents could affect weather patterns. Global ocean currents depend on a process that works like a conveyor belt. They are driven by warm water, which rises to the top of the sea. When this water travels close to the poles—either the Antarctic in the South or the Arctic in the North—it cools off and begins to sink. Melting ice releases huge amounts of freshwater into the saltwater ocean. Because freshwater is more **buoyant**, it can keep the cold water from sinking. In turn, the entire conveyor belt might change in harmful ways.

What would happen then? Believe it or not, some climatologists say temperatures would actually drop 15 to 20 degrees in parts of North America. In Europe, it might snow in the summer. That is one of the misconceptions of global warming. The weather doesn't simply get hotter. In fact, there is evidence that similar weather patterns existed at the end of the last Ice Age. When temperatures warmed and the ice sheets began to melt, the climate reversed direction and became frigid again for more than 1,000 years.

Andreas Peter Ahlstroem, a Dutch environmental expert, has documented how quickly Greenland's Ilulissat glacier has been melting.

One way to measure how fast things are melting is to watch how sea ice is moving. In 2006, a group called the International Polar Year placed a small boat in the sea ice in Eastern Siberia. A century earlier, the same experiment was conducted. Back then, the boat took 34 months to reach Greenland. This time it took 14 months. That was much faster than scientists estimated, which showed them just how quickly the sea ice was melting.

In Greenland, researchers are also watching glaciers. During a normal year, a certain amount of water from glaciers trickles into the ocean. But in recent years, that flow has increased. At the same time, Greenland's surface ice is melting into huge freshwater lakes. This is normal—except that some of these lakes are disappearing overnight. Environmental scientists know that the water is draining into large cracks, or fissures, in the ice. But where does it go from there? The fear is that it may be seeping underneath Greenland's glaciers. This could **lubricate** a giant sheet of ice, which could then slide into the surrounding saltwater.

Some people choose to live in deserts, as in this town in the Sahara.

THE EARTH'S DESERTS

At the planet's other extreme are its deserts. A desert is an extremely dry region that typically gets less than 10 inches (25.4 centimeters) of rain a year. Below that amount, it is very difficult for plants to grow.

The world's largest desert is the Sahara, in North Africa. It covers more than 3 million square miles (7.8 million square kilometers)—and it's growing. This process, called desertification, is one of the most serious problems in environmental science.

Desertification takes place in arid regions, which are also called drylands. In these places, there is already so little water that only the most specialized plants and animals can survive. Around 40 percent of the land on earth can be considered drylands. Roughly 2 billion people live in these areas, and about half of them are threatened by future desertification.

Desertification can be caused by human activity, such as overgrazing of livestock or **slash-and-burn agriculture**. It can also be caused by small changes in the climate. The problem is particularly bad in Africa. According to the United Nations Food and Agriculture Organization, the southern part of the Sahara Desert has grown by 250,000 square miles (647,497 square kilometers) over the past 50 years.

What happens when people, plants, and animals suddenly find their ecosystem pushed to the extreme? The first victim is biodiversity. Some animals and plants simply cannot live in a desert environment.

The stress placed on humans in extremely dry environments can lead to violence. In a local setting, arguments over a few gallons of water can quickly turn deadly. In a larger context, full-scale war can break out. For example, in Africa, the conflicts in Sudan and Somalia during the early 21st century have their roots in tribal disputes that include land with precious water resources. Even worse, this unrest has made the region unstable, allowing terrorists and drug dealers to use remote desert areas as hideouts and **smuggling** routes.

Because of climbing global temperatures, problems caused by extreme environments are likely to get worse before they get better. According to the United Nations Environment Programme, 25 African nations will face severe water problems by 2025. Another U.N. study estimated that 46 percent of the land in Africa is getting drier. Based on what we've seen in the past, these conditions could lead to more human conflict and more damage to ecosystems.

Bright Ideas

WORKING WITH NATURE, NOT AGAINST IT

The earth's population will probably reach 10 billion in your lifetime. At the same time, the climate will continue to change in unpredictable ways. Resources such as food and water will become harder to manage. In turn, humans will have to make the most of extreme environments. And with our help, so will plants and animals. From the ocean floor to outer space, it may not be long before life starts to flourish in places that were once thought to be uninhabitable.

The first step in this journey is to understand the mistakes of the past. Perhaps the greatest one was how we viewed nature. For centuries, humans thought of wind, water, soil, sunshine, animals, and trees as resources they were free to use without consequences. People are beginning to see just how valuable these resources are. That has allowed true problem solving to begin.

A farmer from Niger shows off his grain crop. Several decades ago, people in this African country adopted new agricultural techniques and made their extreme environment work for them.

In extreme environments, these solutions need to work on many different levels at once. However, they do not need to be complicated. For example, in South Africa, the water table—a measurement of the wetness of the ground—is dropping. Meanwhile, farmers are growing crops that need lots of water. These crops are not native to South Africa. A recent project to replace these crops with native ones restored the water table. It also provided jobs for people in poor areas and helped farming to recover in drought-stricken areas.

SAVING TREES

Of course, some solutions are complicated. At least they look complicated at first. For example, some companies that create large amounts of **greenhouse gases** understand that they are partly responsible for climate change. They also understand that climate change can turn a challenging environment into an extreme one.

In 2008, the United Nations started a program called Reducing **Emissions** from Deforestation and Forest **Degradation** (REDD). In this program, companies in **industrialized** countries become partners with farmers in developing countries to save trees. In poor areas where crop production is falling, farmers have to make up for the money they lose. Often, they cut down forests to expose new farmland. Farmers who are part of REDD are

REDD was designed in part to stop illegal logging operations such as this one in Sumatra, an island off the coast of Indonesia.

encouraged to leave trees standing. In fact, they are paid to do so.

Trees absorb and store large amounts of CO_2 as they grow. The goal of REDD is to use the world's trees to soak up CO_2 until more green energy options are available. It is a "win-win-win" situation. Farmers get paid for allowing trees to remain—which requires no extra work. Companies spend less paying these farmers than they would buying expensive machines to capture CO_2 emissions. And the trees that are saved store large amounts of CO_2. If REDD works the way scientists hope, world carbon emissions will be greatly reduced, and billions of dollars will flow into regions that desperately need the money.

FIGHTING BACK

Throughout history, many cultures have thrived in extreme environments. The Inuits and Yupiks (also known as Eskimos) have made their homes in the Arctic for thousands of years. The Berbers (North Africa), Bedouins (Middle East), and Pueblos (American Southwest) have lived for many centuries in the world's hottest, harshest deserts. But what of the people who live on the edge of environments that are being pushed to extremes now? They may not have the skills to adapt.

Wall Flowers

The most extreme environment for plant life is not a burning desert or frozen tundra. It is steel and concrete. That is why cities set aside parks and other areas for seeds to grow and flowers to bloom. Without these places wedged between buildings and sidewalks, cities would be very unhappy places. That is why some architects have taken this idea to the extreme. They are designing structures with vertical gardens—walls of plants and flowers. Some contain more than 200 different species.

When vertical gardens are built correctly, they reduce a building's energy costs. They also encourage wildlife to return to cities. The plastic and metal modules used to create vertical gardens are expensive—in some cases four times more than the ones used for rooftop gardens. Also, they need to be watered, because rain does not fall sideways. Is the added trouble and expense worth it? A look at the smiling faces of the people who live and work around vertical gardens is all you need to know.

Patrick Blanc is one of the world's leading designers of vertical gardens, including this one in Hong Kong.

Can they do so without millions of dollars of government aid?

In the African country of Niger, the people living at the southern edge of the Sahara Desert have. For generations, they watched as the desert slowly swallowed their land. In the 1980s and 1990s, they began making low walls out of sticks and stones and digging shallow ditches. This helped keep their soil from blowing away and caught seeds and insects. When farmers added fertilizer to these patches, they turned the soil into tiny gardening plots, then into narrow fields. They planted tough, desert trees to hold the earth in place and put nutrients back into the soil. Now thousands of acres of barren land have been transformed into fields and forests—and the Sahara has been "pushed back." Vast areas that were once barren are now green. Plants and animals that had not been seen for decades are returning to their restored habitat.

SPACEPORT AMERICA

The most extreme environment of all is outer space. There is no air to breathe, no food to eat, and no water to drink. Without a spacesuit, oxygen would leave your lungs and bloodstream within a few seconds. Without oxygen in your blood, you would die of **hypoxia** within a few minutes. Yet even at the risk of death, humans are eager to explore outer space.

While scientists and engineers work on ways to keep people alive on space journeys, the first spaceport is taking shape in Las Cruces, New Mexico. The project is a partnership between Virgin Galactic and the State of New Mexico. Sometime soon, the age of space tourism will begin. Hundreds of people have already signed up to fly—at a cost of $200,000 or more per ticket. What is the hope? One day, Spaceport America will be a launching point for scientific missions.

5 Trailblazers

These people are doing things to help keep extreme environments safe today...and make the world better for tomorrow.

Ethan Budiansky

Environmentalist

Budiansky works with Trees for the Future, one of many groups that sent people and money to the nation of Haiti after it was rocked by an earthquake in 2010. The disaster devastated the country and focused the spotlight on its health and economic problems. Many of those are linked to deforestation. Budiansky is in charge of an effort to plant thousands of trees in Haiti.

Al Gore

Political Leader

Gore was vice president of the United States in the 1990s. After leaving office, he became the leading voice in the fight against global warming. In 2007, Gore received the Nobel Peace Prize for his work.

Majora Carter

Activist

Carter (above) wants to create good jobs and healthy living spaces for people across the country, including those in environments made extreme by pollution and other human activity. For example, as part of her vision to "green the ghetto" in the South Bronx in New York City, Carter turned an illegal dump into an award-winning waterfront park.

Kevin Glover

Geneticist

As a geneticist, Glover studies the **heredity** of plants and animals. He discovered that a species of Antarctic whale was migrating all the way to the Arctic. His finding added an important piece of evidence to the belief that there may be big problems with the food chain in Antarctica's waters.

6 Field Tested

orking in extreme environments does not mean you have to work under extreme conditions. In recent years, many countries have come to understand that scientists and researchers are at their best when they have a few of the comforts of home. They have invested money to design and build new facilities in areas with extreme weather. Nowhere has this change been more noticeable than in Antarctica. The drafty old shacks and huts that used to house scientific teams have been replaced by futuristic research stations.

The first facility of this kind was built in 1997 by South Africa. Sanae IV sits on a ledge 800 feet (244 meters) high and can house 10 people at a time. The staff changes every 15 months. England's Halley VI sits in the exact location where scientists first detected a hole in the **ozone** layer. That makes it the perfect place to watch future changes in Earth's atmosphere.

The United States South Pole Station is huge—it holds up to 150 people. It is designed like an airplane wing. Air going underneath it goes faster than the air above it. That keeps it from being buried by snow. One of the newest stations is Belgium's Princess Elizabeth. It is Antarctica's first "green" outpost—it is nearly 100 percent free of carbon.

Explorer Alain Hubert walks the grounds of Belgium's Princess Elizabeth station.

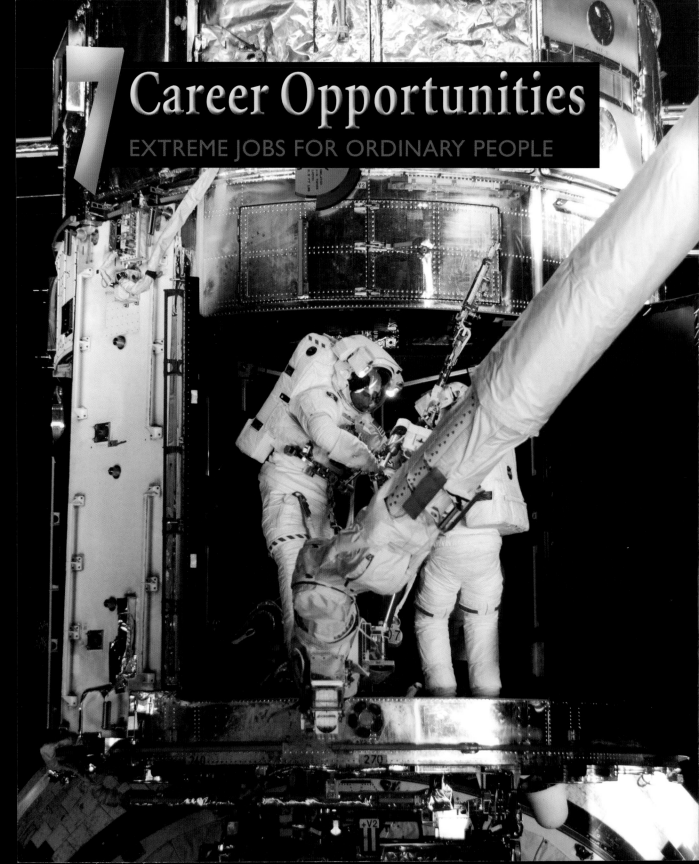

7 Career Opportunities

EXTREME JOBS FOR ORDINARY PEOPLE

Working in extreme environments is not for everyone. There are many dangers and challenges. Some wonder why people would put themselves in harm's way in the first place. The answer is that understanding ecosystems on the edge has great value. Indeed, the more we know about these places, the more we learn about how our planet works. Also, studying environments that have become extreme due to human activity will hopefully keep us from repeating our mistakes in the future.

TEAM PLAYERS

Most people working in extreme environments are part of a partnership. For example, a team trying to improve farming in arid regions would almost certainly include an expert on **sustainable agriculture**. It might also include a climatologist, engineer, and anthropologist. The climatologist would study weather patterns. The engineer would design new tools or machines for the farmers. And the anthropologist would find the best way to fit new farming techniques into the existing culture.

In their search to learn more about our planet, some scientists are studying the extreme conditions of outer space.

Genetic researchers also work together in teams. They are interested in extreme environments because of the way plants and animals survive harsh conditions. They know that cells under great stress have the ability to correct damage to their DNA (deoxyribonucleic acid). DNA is the "instruction manual" for the cells that make up all living things.

If DNA is not repaired, the result can be a mutation—a change to the instruction manual that is passed on to the next generation. Extreme environments give research teams a great place to study DNA. In searching for important genetic clues, they often test theories and look for answers in extreme climates.

STAR GAZERS

No climate on earth can exactly match the extremes of outer space. In fact, many people believe the next great human adventure will be the search for **extraterrestrial** life. That is why many scientists are interested in the field of astrobiology. They study life in extreme environments on earth to understand what we might find in the extreme environments on other planets.

In astrobiology, scientists sometimes try to understand how **microbes** and **bacteria** react under conditions even more extreme than on earth. In 2011, an experiment was carried out by the Japan Agency for Marine-Earth Science and Technology.

Four types of bacteria were exposed to more than 400,000 times the gravity of earth. These forces might exist close to a star like our sun. All four bacteria survived, and two even grew—including *E. coli*, a bacteria in your intestines.

This was exciting news. Some scientists believe that life on earth started when microbes "hitchhiked" on rocks created by explosions on other planets. The experiment in Japan proved that microbes could survive the forces of that explosion. Anyone who ever wondered why people would study extreme environments had a fantastic answer.

Extremophiles

Some scientists have devoted themselves to the study of microorganisms that survive in the most extreme environments. This grouping is called extremophiles. The places they live are so hot, so cold, or so acidic that it is hard to imagine how anything could survive in such conditions. One of the best-known extremophiles is the water bear. This tiny, eight-legged microorganism can live in temperatures that would kill almost anything else. In 2007, Russian scientists exposed water bears to outer space for 10 days. Many survived and were able to reproduce!

Some extremophiles are even more amazing than the water bear. In 2010, the National Aeronautics and Space Administration (NASA) showed that certain extremophiles could use the toxic substance arsenic as a building block. This discovery wasn't made in outer space—it was made on earth, in Yellowstone Park!

This is how a water bear looks under the microscope.

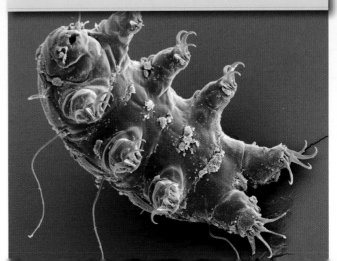

8 Expert Opinions

When the best minds talk about extreme environments, it's worth listening to what they say...

"Just like any garden, maintaining a green wall takes commitment. It shouldn't be considered a building material, but more like a pet."

> —*Minsuk Cho, architect, on vertical gardens*

"I think the environment should be put in the category of our national security. Defense of our resources is just as important as defense abroad. Otherwise what is there to defend?"

> —*Robert Redford, actor and environmentalist, on what the government should do to protect the environment*

"Planting trees is not just some quaint side project. It's the key to rebuilding the country."

> —*Helen Clark, United Nations official, on the work being done to fix Haiti's environmental damage*

"It was the biggest environmental transformation in Africa."

> —*Chris Reij, Dutch researcher, on efforts to turn back the desert in Niger*

Sylvia Earle enjoys the view from a Deep Worker Sub,
a vessel designed for underwater studies.

"In our schools we are focusing on numbers and letters
but we need, from the earliest times, to get across the
concept that we are connected to nature and that we are
trying to find a space to sustain ourselves."

*—Sylvia Earle, oceanographer, on the importance
of living in concert with nature*

"We face a genuine planetary emergency…we cannot just
talk about it, we have to act on it, we have to solve it—
urgently."

*—Al Gore, politician and environmentalist, on
getting to work on environmental problems*

9

What Can I Do?

Most kids in North America don't live near an extreme environment. But that doesn't mean you should ignore high-stress ecosystems. Learning about them will help you understand how the earth's environments are connected and whether humans can survive in them. Remember what happens in a remote area could impact your corner of the world some day.

There are lots of ways to increase your knowledge. For example, you can track the weather in your town and compare it to other areas of the country or the world. You can also connect with a young person who lives in or near an extreme environment. Kids who deal with environmental stress have a very different daily life than you do. You can communicate with them as a "pen pal." Children in different parts of the world have been sharing their experiences in this way for many decades. Every few weeks or months, they send letters back and forth. When pen pals get older, they often visit each other.

To find a pen pal, you'll need permission from a parent. Then you can join a program that will help you find a friend in an extreme environment. Be prepared to dust off your letter-writing skills—your pen pal may not have access to a computer. By learning how people deal with the challenges of extreme environments, you may just end up discovering something that makes our planet a safer, happier place.

One way to find out more about extreme environments is by starting a letter-writing relationship with a pen pal.

Glossary

Anthropologists—People who study humans and their evolution.

Arthropod—An insect with a segmented body and jointed arms and legs.

Bacteria—Single-celled microorganisms that live in soil, water, or bodies of plants and animals.

Biodiversity—The number and variety of plant and animal species in a certain place.

Buoyant—Able to float.

Climate Change—A long-term change in weather conditions.

Degradation—Lessening in value, strength, or quality.

Ecosystems—All the organisms, plants, and animals that make up specific ecological areas.

Emissions—Substances discharged into the air.

Extraterrestrial—Not from our planet.

Greenhouse Gases—Gases that trap heat in the atmosphere, just as a greenhouse does during the winter.

Heredity—All the genetic characteristics derived from ancestors.

Hypoxia—Not enough oxygen reaching muscle tissue.

Industrialized—Dependent on factories, businesses, and agriculture to create jobs and revenues.

Irrigation—Systems designed for watering crops.

Limestone—A rock that is often used in building.

Lubricate—Make slippery or smooth.

Microbes—Another term for microorganisms or germs.

Monsoon—A period of extremely heavy rainfall.

Organic—Produced naturally, without the help of pesticides or chemical fertilizers.

Ozone—A form of oxygen that is helpful to the upper atmosphere.

Rituals—Actions that are always performed in the same order.

Slash-and-Burn Agriculture—A farming technique that clears forests by burning them down.

Smuggling—Taking and transporting something secretly and illegally.

Sustainable Agriculture—Farming techniques that use resources in a way that also helps replenish them.

Water Management—The ways that a town, city, or country uses water.

Sources

The authors relied on many different books, magazines, and organizations to do research for this book. Listed below are the primary sources of information and their websites:

Discover Magazine — www.discovermagazine.com
National Geographic Magazine — www.nationalgeographic.com
National Snow and Ice Data Center — www.nsidc.org
The New York Times — www.nytimes.com
Newsweek Magazine — www.newsweek.com
Seed Magazine — www.seedmagazine.com
Science Magazine — www.sciencemag.org
Science News — www.sciencenews.org
Time Magazine — www.time.com

Resources

To get involved with efforts to help the environment, you can contact these organizations:

Academy of Natural Sciences — www.ansp.org
The Astrobiology Web — www.astrobiology.com
The Living Desert — www.livingdesert.org
Natural History Museum/London — www.nhm.ac.uk
Science Daily — www.sciencedaily.com

For more information on the subjects covered in this book:

Gritzner, Charles F. *Polar Regions*. New York, New York. Chelsea House, 2006.

Kiesbye, Stefan. *Are Natural Disasters Increasing?* Farmington Hills, Michigan. Greenhaven Press, 2010.

Nardo, Don. *Extreme Threats: Climate Change.* Greensboro, North Carolina. Morgan Reynolds Publishing, 2009.

Index

Page numbers in **bold** refer to illustrations.

Ahlstroem, Andreas Peter....**25**
Antarctica....13, 23, 24, 35, 37
Arctic....**22**, 24, 31, 35
Army Corps of Engineers....5
Atacama Desert....7, **7**, 8
Atlantic Ocean....17

Babylonians....19
Bedouins....31
Berbers....31
Birds Point levee....5
Budiansky, Ethan....34

Carter, Majora....35, **35**
Cho, Minsuk....42
Clark, Helen....42

Earle, Sylvia....43, **43**
Eocene Epoch....17
Eskimos....31
Euphrates River....19, 20

Fertile Crescent, The....19, 20

Glover, Kevin....35
Gore, Al....34, 43

Halley VI station....37
Hubert, Alain....**36**
Hurricane Katrina....10

Ice Age....18, 24
Indus River....6
International Polar Year....25
Inuits....31

Mars....7
Mayans....21
Mississippi River....5, 6, 10

National Aeronautics and
    Space Administration
    (NASA)....41
Neanderthals....18, **18**, 19

Parthians....19
Passerine....8
Princess Elizabeth
    station....**36**, 37
Pueblos....31

Redford, Robert....42
Reducing Emissions from
    Deforestation and
    Forest Degradation
    (REDD)....30, 31
Reij, Chris....42
Ring of Fire....10

Sahara Desert....26, **26**, 27, 33
Sanae IV station....37
Sumerians....19

Tigris River....19, 20
Trees for the Future....34
Tungurahua volcano....**14**

United Nations....27, 30, 42
United Nations Environment
    Programme....27
United Nations
    Food and Agriculture
    Organization....27
United States South
    Pole Station....37

Virgin Galactic....33

Water Bear....41, **41**

Yellowstone Park....41
Yupiks....31

The Authors

AMY K. TILMONT is a science teacher at The Rumson Country Day School in Rumson, New Jersey. She is a graduate of Lycoming College. Her areas of expertise include Geology and Environmental Science.

JEFFREY R. GARSIDE is also a science teacher at The Rumson Country Day School. He graduated from Northeastern University and holds a Masters degree from Kean College. Jeff teaches Chemistry, Physics and Biology, and is head of RCDS's Science Department.

MARK STEWART has written more than 200 non-fiction books for the school and library market. He has an undergraduate degree in History from Duke University. Mark's work in environmental studies includes books on the plants and animals of New York (where he grew up) and New Jersey (where he lives now).